PRINCIPALITY OF LIECHTENSTEIN
EXPERIENCE – A JOURNEY IN PICTURES

PRINCIPALITY OF LIECHTENSTEIN

EXPERIENCE – A JOURNEY IN PICTURES

Acknowledgement

I thank the following warmly for their assistance and valuable suggestions in the preparation of this book: Hereditary Prince Alois, Prime Minister Otmar Hasler, Dr. Gerlinde Manz-Christ, Daniela Clavadetscher, Wilfried Hoop, Roland Büchel, Michael Gattenhof, Josef Beck, Mike Lauber and numerous others. Special thanks are due to Egon Gstöhl for editing the text, the photographic team Roland Korner and Wolfgang Müller and the staff of Druckerei Gutenberg AG.

Marco Nescher, publisher

National Library of Germany bibliographical details

The National Library of Germany lists this publication in the German National Bibliography; detailed bibliographical data may be accessed on the internet at http://dnb.ddb.de.

2nd edition 2006
© 2005 Alpenland Verlag AG, Schaan

Publisher: Marco Nescher, Schaan
Text: Egon Gstöhl, promedia, Eschen
English translation: hilty übersetzungen, Schaan
Photographs: Roland Korner and Wolfgang Müller, Close up AG, Triesen
Reproductions: Page 19: National Archives; Page 156: Raiffeisenbank Liechtenstein AG
Layout: Andy Crestani, Gutenberg AG, Schaan
Typesetting and lithography: Gutenberg AG, Schaan
Font: Rotis Sans Serif, Rotis Semi Serif
Printing: Gutenberg AG, Schaan
Paper: Magno Satin 170 g/m² supplied by Sihl+Eika Papier AG, Thalwil, www.papier.ch
Publishing house: Alpenland Verlag AG, Feldkircher Strasse 13, FL-9494 Schaan
Internet: www.alpenlandverlag.li, www.buchzentrum.li

ISBN 3-905437-10-4

Table of contents

7	**Foreword by Hereditary Prince Alois von und zu Liechtenstein**
10	**Introduction**
	Liechtenstein – Relativity of smallness – Sovereignty
16	**Princely House**
	Princely Family – Continuity – Hereditary Prince Alois – Princely House – Vaduz Castle
32	**Liechtenstein Museum in Vienna**
	World renown – Highlights
38	**Politics**
	Integration – National policy – Democracy – Self-determination – Media – Knowledge
50	**Industry**
	Enterprise – Diversification – Ahead in knowledge – Internationality – Orientation towards Switzerland – Economic agreements – Value creation – Locational policy – Brands
72	**Manufacturing and service industries**
	Small businesses – Apprentice training
76	**Financial centre**
	Intersection points – Financial centre – Banking secrecy
82	**Agriculture**
	Milk production – Organic products
88	**Culinary matters**
	Winegrowing – Haute cuisine – Specialities – Scene
96	**Art, culture and history**
	Country of culture – Artists – Museum of Fine Arts – National Museum – Stamps
108	**Leisure and tourism**
	Quality of life – Movement – Family paradise
118	**Villages**
	Rhine culture – Historic buildings – Architecture – Geography – Traditions – Local autonomy – Houses of God – Patronage – Moods
150	**Neighbourhood**
	Werdenberg – Feldkirch – Maienfeld
156	**Panoramic map of Liechtenstein**
158	**Bibliography**
159	**Landmarks in Liechtenstein history**
160	**Addresses and internet sites**

A vision for Liechtenstein

«Experiencing Liechtenstein» is the idea behind this book of photographs. It contains snapshots of our remarkable country, delineating the modern small state – its political, economic, cultural and scenic diversity in a changing world. Liechtenstein is well placed in the international competition between business locations. Favourable economic data, a policy of active integration and a stable political framework give us a good starting position. It is however becoming clear that after a sustained boom period bold reforms are required if we are to continue into a successful future. The state must concentrate on its essential functions, acting in a supporting role and with transparent structures. The scope for action also extends to our financial and taxation systems, to administration and to education. Further development in these important areas will strengthen us as a business location. To cope with the major challenges of our times, an ageing society and public-sector budgets which have come under increasing strain, we must however act not just correctly but also in good time. The internationally acknowledged reforms to our financial centre have shown us how important the time factor is.

Continuity in the monarchy and the monarch's independence allow a keener eye to be kept on the broad fundamentals of policy. This monarchical element in Liechtenstein's direct democracy is the modern embodiment of hereditary monarchy on a democratic and parliamentary foundation. Shared responsibility, as our dualistic Constitution lays down, is reciprocally complementary and makes us strong. For smallness can be a positive advantage if the opportunities it presents are correctly exploited. Liechtenstein has always understood this well because it has had something of inestimable value to build on: friendly states and dependable partners, as reflected in the especially close relations with our neighbours Switzerland and Austria. I hope that this book may help Liechtenstein to make new friends and be perceived as a cooperative small state which is fully committed to the international community.

Hereditary Prince Alois
von und zu Liechtenstein

The vista from the Eschnerberg rise over the community of Eschen-Nendeln in the Liechtenstein Unterland displays the rural character of the picturesque landscape. In the background the village of Nendeln can be seen on the left and, above it, the mountain community of Planken at the foot of the Three Sisters massif.

Liechtenstein – small state and monarchy with European flair

The Rhine as the natural border between two friendly states. Liechtenstein is bound to Switzerland by much more than just the joint economic and currency area.

The hospitable country is familiar to art-lovers from near and far.

With a territory of 160 square kilometres the Principality of Liechtenstein is the fourth smallest country in Europe. A remarkable country forming a state with 35,000 people. Politically unique, it combines well-developed popular rights under direct democracy with the distinctive features of monarchy as a system of government. Continuity and predictability in foreign policy have earned the sovereign and cosmopolitan small state international recognition. In the community of states the Principality stands for tolerant coexistence and the right of nations to self-determination. For small states above all need interchange with and stimuli from outside to be able to surmount their natural borders and utilise their opportunities. Ingenious minds in Liechtenstein realised long ago that borders not only divide, but also unite. The country's great economic upsurge is not least a result of this opening up and close cooperation with adjoining countries. A special position is taken here by the friendly-neighbour relations with Switzerland, with which Liechtenstein forms a customs and currency union.

Symbol of political Liechtenstein: the Government Building in Vaduz decked with a flag in the national colours is the official seat of the five-member Government and the place where Parliament meets.

Relativity of smallness – knowledge surmounts borders

View of the Principality of Liechtenstein from the Swiss side of the Rhine valley.

Swiss customs officials perform their duties on the border with EU-state Austria.

Liechtenstein is compact. There are even athletes capable of covering its outer limits on foot in a day. But this geographical smallness is relative. Whenever countries are compared per head of population, Liechtenstein is always amongst the foremost. Intelligent interaction between politics and economics, exploitation of locational advantages and intensive transfer of knowledge have turned Liechtenstein into an industrial and service-providing country. Its first-rate economic and financial data reflect its strong internationalisation. Working affiliations with adjoining countries form an important part of Liechtenstein's basis as a business location.

Seven Rhine bridges link Liechtenstein with Switzerland. The open frontier epitomises the partnership between the two countries, which cooperate closely in many areas.

Sovereignty – eleven communities form an independent state

The Great State coat of arms

Gamprin

Schellenberg

Planken

Eschen

Ruggell

Mauren

Schaan

Triesenberg

Vaduz

Balzers

Triesen

The key values in the Constitution reflect the country's sovereign statehood. In 1806 Liechtenstein acquired sovereignty by inclusion in the Federation of the Rhine. The banking centre is considered the essence of stability and trust. Liechtenstein is, however, also a country of culture and art, a scenic jewel. Many of the familiar pictures which constitute the country's image in the world do it less than justice. They show only individual elements in this fascinating mixture of natural paradise and centre of business, of rural character and urban facilities, of monarchy and direct democracy with a high degree of political self-determination for the eleven local communities. Diversity in microcosm and the charm of the individual are among Liechtenstein's important characteristics.

The coats of arms of Liechtenstein's eleven local communities (above) and the Great State coat of arms on the front of the Government Building represent the supreme political authorities.

The silhouette of Vaduz Castle, first mentioned in 1322, evokes the eventful history of the former County of Vaduz which passed to the Princely House of Liechtenstein in 1712.

Liechtenstein – the Princes and the land on the young Rhine

Witness to an eventful history: canon at the entrance to the inner courtyard of Vaduz Castle.

The coat of arms of the reigning Princely House with its escutcheon in gold and red.

The name Liechtenstein is closely bound up with European politics and history. The House of Liechtenstein is one of the oldest noble families. A bearer of this name, Hugo von Liechtenstein, is first mentioned in about 1136. In 1608 Karl von Liechtenstein was the first member of the family to acquire the rank of Hereditary Prince. In 1606 he concluded with his brothers Maximilian and Gundaker a Family Covenant which accorded the right to the hereditary title to the first-born of the eldest line. In 1993 this Covenant was subsumed together with additional rules in the new House Statute, which forms the basis of the succession law now operative in Liechtenstein.

Ever since the rank of Imperial Prince was attained the House of Liechtenstein had sought to acquire a territory which was an immediate fief of the Empire. But it was not until the time of Karl's grandson Prince Johann Adam Andreas that the opportunity finally arose to purchase the Lordship of Schellenberg in 1699 and the County of Vaduz in 1712. Under the imperial charter of 23rd January 1719 these two territories were united and elevated by the Emperor Karl VI to form the Imperial Principality of Liechtenstein. Until 1938 the Princes of Liechtenstein lived in Vienna and Moravia. They held important military and diplomatic posts for the Habsburg monarchy and administered their extensive estates in Lower Austria, Bohemia, Silesia and Moravia. Its adroit political moves earned the House, which was also well-disposed towards art and science, high regard. Increasingly the dynasty showed itself able to combine tradition with the demands of altered times. Precisely that is perhaps the great strength of the monarchy in Liechtenstein, which has officially borne the Princely Family's name since 1719. In the mid-19th century Liechtenstein acquired its first Constitution, which was given strengthened popular rights in 1862 and 1921 and has led to the present-day form of «constitutional hereditary monarchy on a democratic and parliamentary foundation». In the most recent constitutional reform of 2003 too the definition of political balance in the interaction between the dual sovereigns Prince and People was to the fore.

Prince Johann Adam Andreas von Liechtenstein laid the foundation for the small state's formation by purchasing its two constituent territories.

The Liechtensteins – first family in the hereditary monarchy

The Hereditary Prince and Princess embody the future of the monarchy in Liechtenstein: Hereditary Prince Alois and Hereditary Princess Sophie.

The Princely couple in the company of their grandchildren – (from left) Princess Marie Caroline, Prince Nikolaus, Prince Georg and Prince Joseph Wenzel.

The Prince is the governor of the Princely House and in accordance with the House Statute guards the «reputation, honour and welfare» of the family, which now numbers over a hundred members. After the death of Prince Franz Josef II on 13th November 1989 Prince Hans-Adam II took charge as the 13th Prince since Liechtenstein's elevation to the status of immediate Imperial Principality in 1719. On 15th August 2004 Hereditary Prince Alois, in preparation for his succession to the throne, took on the duties of Head of State as deputy for the Reigning Prince: «The general directions and fundamental political issues for which I stand as independent Head of State for the good of all citizens are what concern me. I would like to ensure continuity with the work done by my father. In some respects however we face different challenges today», says the Hereditary Prince, with an eye to the future.

Vaduz Castle is the symbol of Liechtenstein and of its monarchy too. It has served as the Princely Family's home since 1938.

Continuity – mission and commitment across the generations

Prince Hans-Adam and Princess Marie von und zu Liechtenstein. Three generations – the Prince, the Hereditary Prince and Prince Joseph Wenzel.

Under the House Statute the Hereditary Prince as the eldest son of the Reigning Prince is the designated successor to the throne. He has therefore been prepared since early youth for his future duties as Head of State, which he has performed as his father's deputy since 2004. After passing the «Matura» school-leaving examination at the Liechtenstein Grammar School he entered the Royal Military Academy at Sandhurst (Gt. Britain), where he completed officer training as Second Lieutenant. For six months he served with the Coldstream Guards in Hong Kong and London. Afterwards he studied jurisprudence at the University of Salzburg, graduating in 1993; this was followed by several years' work for a firm of chartered accountants in London and the performing of various duties in the administration of the princely estates. On 3rd July 1993 Hereditary Prince Alois von und zu Liechtenstein married Duchess Sophie in Bayern. On 24th May 1995 the first-born son of the Hereditary Prince and Princess and heir to the throne Prince Joseph Wenzel was born. His sister and brothers are Princess Marie Caroline, born on 17th October 1996, Prince Georg, born on 20th April 1999, and Prince Nikolaus, born on 6th December 2000. The families of the Prince and Hereditary Prince represent three generations of Liechtenstein's contemporary-style monarchy, which as a link between tradition and future gives the small state continuity and political stability.

The Hereditary Prince and his family: (from left) Prince Georg, Hereditary Prince Alois, Princess Marie Caroline, Hereditary Princess Sophie, Prince Joseph Wenzel and Prince Nikolaus.

Hereditary Prince Alois – the deputy on the way to the throne

Outdoor Mass on the Castle meadow on the National Holiday, 15th August.

Arrival of the Princely Family.

Official address by the Hereditary Prince.

The Hereditary Prince represents the younger generation, is extremely well-educated and is conscious of the traditions and values of the House. And yet he is very open to new ideas and, thanks to his experience abroad, discriminating. His holistic outlook, a dash of pragmatism and a mixture of aristocratic reserve and winning self-assurance constitute his appeal. «A modern monarch in a politically active monarchy such as we have here in Liechtenstein should find the time to reflect deeply on the long-term challenges facing the state, and then at the right time speak clearly about necessary reforms.» This political creed of the Hereditary Prince calls not just for analytical and strategic skills, but above all for an independent mind. «This independence of other state institutions is essential if the Head of State is to be capable of occasionally intervening correctively for the good of the minority against ‹dictatorship› by the majority.»

Popular and close to the people: the members of the Princely House are held in high esteem.

A high point in Liechtenstein's National Holiday is the spectacular firework display held in the Castle gardens.

Princely House – the monarchy in direct democracy

Direct democracy in Liechtenstein and the high degree of self-determination enjoyed by the communities are very important to the Hereditary Prince. In his first official speech as deputy for the Reigning Prince he advocated strengthening the autonomy of the local communities. «Decisions are best when they are made as close to the people as possible. My family's concept of governance has concentrated on the essentials, in that we have for example always favoured a liberal economic policy confined to providing good training and establishing a helpful framework. We also strongly supported Liechtenstein's internationalisation, which led ultimately to accession to the UNO and EEA.»

President Fischer of Austria is cordially welcomed by Hereditary Princess Sophie. The distinguished guest is awarded the Princely Liechtenstein Order of Merit.

Official visits by foreign state guests lead to Vaduz Castle.

Tranquil fountain in the Castle courtyard, an architectural jewel which immediately captivates visitors.

The inner courtyard of Vaduz Castle with its charming corners and fine facades radiates tranquillity and harmony.

Vaduz Castle – symbol and seat of the Princely Family

Works of art from the collections adorn the Princely Family's living quarters.

The Library, like the Staircase Hall pictured on the following double page, is one of the Castle's most beautiful rooms and is used for receptions.

Vaduz Castle, the first documentary mention of which dates from 1322, tells an eventful story of the country's earlier rulers, the Counts of Werdenberg zu Vaduz, the Barons of Brandis from the Emmental, the Counts of Sulz from Klettgau in Baden and the Counts of Hohenems from Vorarlberg. But the historic building also bears witness to having been variously used after passing in 1712 to the Princes of Liechtenstein, then resident in Vienna. Before the Castle became the residence of the then Reigning Prince Franz Josef II in 1938, parts of it were used as office buildings, barracks and a restaurant. Today, restored with stylistic integrity and with its characteristic and enchanting inner courtyards and living accommodation, the Castle is both the family home of the Prince and Hereditary Prince and the official residence of Liechtenstein's Head of State. Dignitaries visiting the state and its political decision-makers are received at Vaduz Castle as the culmination of their stay. The Castle is the embodiment of the Liechtenstein form of government, a symbol of Liechtenstein visible from afar on the mountain slope rising above Vaduz. As a symbol of the monarchy it represents continuity across the generations.

The interplay of mediaeval construction and contemporary comfort and convenience are what give Vaduz Castle its special appeal.

World renown – art treasures in Vaduz and Vienna

The Liechtenstein Museum has been a magnet in the Viennese cultural landscape since its opening in 2004.

The Princely Family of Liechtenstein has for generations been united by its love of art. Some of the unique art treasures belonging to the Princely House of Liechtenstein have returned from Vaduz to Vienna – to a place in the cultural capital of Europe which unites most perfectly the historical ambience of the Princely Family and the centuries-old tradition of the Princely House as collector and patron of the arts, the Garden Palace in Rossau, Vienna.

The Garden Palace now used as a museum was built in the Viennese district of Rossau under Prince Johann Adam Andreas I von Liechtenstein (1657–1712).

Highlights – showpieces of breathtaking beauty

Prince Hans-Adam II takes pleasure in the Palace's successful conversion into a jewel among European art museums.

Paintings, sculptures and furniture in the baroque Garden Palace form a uniquely concentrated atmosphere.

The opening of the Liechtenstein Museum has given culture- and art-spoiled Vienna a new highlight. It resurrects an old tradition. For as long ago as 1806 the Princely House opened the doors of the Garden Palace in the Viennese district of Rossau to the public to display showpieces from the collections. In 1938 it was closed. The sections from the Princely Collections fascinate and delight art-lovers from all over the world. With their breathtaking artistic quality and diversity these works of art spanning four centuries are rated one of the world's most important and beautiful private collections. The exquisite treasures added to the collection with great artistic sensibility since the 17th century are presented in Vienna as an ensemble on the lines of the classical Temple of the Muses. The objets d'art originally acquired to adorn the numerous castles of the Princes of Liechtenstein are displayed as an integrated artwork. Paintings, sculptures, ornamental pieces and furniture form an imposing unity which reflects the atmosphere of the Princely Family's baroque summer residence.

The Museum building with its furnishings and the objects from the collection are displayed as an integrated artwork.

Integration – committed cooperation with Europe and the world

 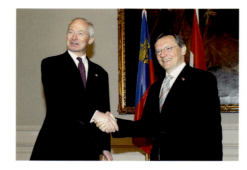 

Ambassador Claudia Fritsche represents Liechtenstein's interests in Washington. Prince Hans-Adam II meets Austrian Chancellor Wolfgang Schüssel in Vienna. Prime Minister Otmar Hasler receives Swiss Federal Councillor Christoph Blocher.

Liechtenstein is present on Europe's political debating floor.

Liechtenstein's Ambassador in Berlin Dr. Josef Wolf.

Liechtenstein is fully committed internationally in the field of human rights and to the further development of international law, to cooperation in development, humanitarian aid and environment policy. Exchange and cooperation are vital to the small state. Liechtenstein therefore cooperates with the international community and contributes to meeting new challenges such as combating both money laundering and the financing of terrorism. Liechtenstein is actively involved in the Organisation for Security and Co-operation in Europe (OSCE) and in the Council of Europe. Economically Liechtenstein is integrated in EFTA, the EEA and the World Trade Organisation (WTO). It also defends its interests as a full member of the UNO and supports there the right of self-determination of nations, tolerance and solidarity.

European cooperation as a member of the OSCE and EEA.

Prince Hans-Adam II von und zu Liechtenstein and Austrian President Thomas Klestil on the occasion of the Prince's official visit to Vienna in 2004.

National policy – safeguarding interests and coping with smallness

At the parliamentary elections the people of Liechtenstein determine the composition of Parliament. Candidates from all three of the country's parties offer themselves for election.

Coalition government: (from left) Minister Dr. Martin Meyer (FBP), Minister Rita Kieber-Beck (FBP), Prime Minister Otmar Hasler (FBP), Deputy Prime Minister Dr. Klaus Tschütscher (VU), Minister Hugo Quaderer (VU).

Every four years Liechtenstein elects the 25 Members of Parliament. All three Liechtenstein parties are represented: the Progressive Citizens' Party (FBP), the Patriotic Union (VU) and the Free List (FL). The legislature elects the five Members of the Government, who are formally appointed to this office by the Prince. This collaboration between monarch and people characterises the Liechtenstein system. Another of its cardinal features is the right to an initiative or referendum. As few as 1000 voters or three communities can demand a referendum. Clarity, direct democracy and autonomy of the local communities promote identification with the state, which depends on the part-time involvement of citizens in public offices.

Hereditary Prince Alois opens Parliament on 14th April 2005 with the traditional speech from the throne, acting for the first time as deputy for the Reigning Prince.

Democracy – parliamentary election und plebiscites

The Members of Parliament in front of the Government Building decked with flags in the national colours blue and red and the gold and red of the Prince. In the electoral period 2005–2009 the FBP holds twelve, the VU ten and the FL three of the twenty-five parliamentary seats.

Liechtenstein's two historic territories form two electoral districts. Of the twenty-five Members of Parliament fifteen are elected in the Oberland, the former County of Vaduz, and ten in the Unterland, the former Lordship of Schellenberg. In the collegiate government the two popular parties FBP und VU, conservative in values and liberal in social policies, form a large coalition, while the Free List is represented only in Parliament as an opposition party. The people of Liechtenstein are asked for their opinions on important issues – when Parliament elects to hold a referendum or when politically committed citizens avail themselves of the right to demand an initiative or referendum.

As a «working parliament» the Liechtenstein Parliament normally debates draft legislation in plenary session.

Self-determination – sovereignty with limited resources

Despite its geographical smallness Liechtenstein performs all its governmental functions itself. In important areas such as the education and health systems there are however cooperation agreements with Switzerland and with Austria.

Office building of the Liechtenstein National Public Administration in Vaduz.

Malicious tongues maintain that Liechtenstein consists entirely of limits. This is a reference to the distinctive fact that from almost any elevated location there is a view into the adjoining neighbourhood. But it is also an allusion to the limited resources. Herein lies a fundamental problem for small states, which have essentially the same problems to solve as large ones – but with fewer people. Liechtenstein meets this challenge with much pragmatism and cooperation at government and administrative level. Advancing internationalisation makes heavy demands on the comparatively small and efficient administration. In just under 50 public offices it puts into effect the constitutional state's Acts of Parliament and executive orders and the obligations entered into by it under international agreements. For performing these tasks the state has at its disposal an annual budget of 900 million francs.

Increasing private transport is a major challenge for Liechtenstein.

Public transport is provided by the lime-green buses of the Liechtenstein Bus Corporation (LBA).

Media – the «fourth estate» in the country as its opinion-formers

Liechtenstein publications: Liechtensteiner Vaterland, Liechtensteiner Volksblatt and the weekly paper LIEWO.

Liechtenstein produces a wide variety of publications every year.

In Liechtenstein, as in other western democracies, opinion is formed through parties and interest groups. A distinctive feature is the commitment and intensity with which political debates are conducted. This is linked to proximity to the state and its representatives, because in small-state circumstances with around 20,000 voters people are often personally acquainted. In the exchange of arguments and points of view an important part is played by the media. Two daily papers appear in Liechtenstein, giving information about what is happening in the country and addressing political topics. Both papers are closely linked to one of the two big parties, the Patriotic Union and the Progressive Citizens' Party. The «FL-Info», a forum for Liechtenstein's third party the Free List, appears quarterly. The country's only independent and up-to-the-minute medium is Radio Liechtenstein, also received elsewhere in the region as the voice of Liechtenstein. The decision-making processes are laid down in the Constitution and find expression in the definition of Liechtenstein's system of government as a «constitutional hereditary monarchy on a democratic and parliamentary foundation». The dualistic Constitution sets out the guidelines for collaboration between the dual sovereigns Prince and People. At national level the political authorities Prince, Parliament and Government together with direct democratic decisions by the population determine the course of policy. Decision-making by the local communities in their own sphere of activity is largely autonomous.

Broadcasts by the national radio station Radio Liechtenstein are received throughout the region from Lake Constance to the Walensee.

Knowledge – education as a strategic success for the state

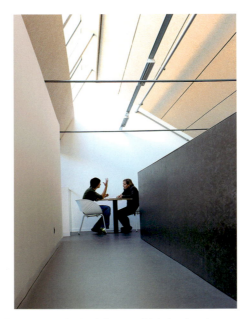

Students at the Liechtenstein University of Applied Sciences receive training at a high level and sought-after diplomas.

Scientific work on the University campus in the Architecture and Economics study programmes.

Knowledge and the application of knowledge are the key to tomorrow's economic success. A high standard of training, steady improvement and adaptation of the education system and knowledge transfer between school and the business world are embedded in Liechtenstein's economic and education policy. Liechtenstein, which has hardly any natural resources, can secure comparative advantages only by intelligent management of knowledge. The education system accordingly ranks high, as also evidenced by the fact that Liechtenstein devotes some 15 percent of its public expenditure to this area. The universal and well-developed school system, establishments of higher education and scientific institutes, together with an adult-education system geared towards life-long learning, are the foundation for the good quality of basic and advanced education and training. In vocational and tertiary-level training Liechtenstein cooperates with neighbouring Switzerland and Austria.

With its practice-oriented study concept the internationally recognised University attracts many students from abroad.

Children theatre
Markt
Butterfly festival
Str... ...sicians, local
... station

Liechtenstein's highly industrialised economy fits into the landscape harmoniously, as this dramatic contrast of high-tech industry and mediaeval castle in Balzers shows.

Enterprise – high-tech, niche-market products and creation of jobs

 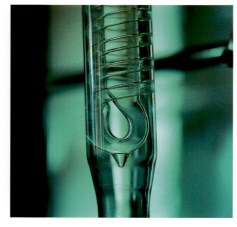 

Thin-film and vacuum technologies from Balzers are opening up new worlds in developing the applications of tomorrow.

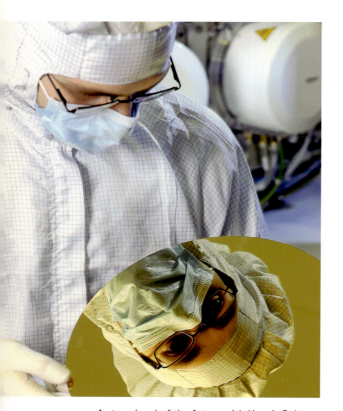

A step ahead of the future with Unaxis Balzers.

There is a tradition of free enterprise in Liechtenstein. The country's liberal economic policy creates a climate which encourages investment and innovation. Good underlying conditions, access to a regional pool of highly-qualified labour, the customs and currency union with Switzerland and parallel membership of the European Economic Area are conducive to economic development. Niche-product policy, a high degree of specialisation and close cooperation with leading universities are sources of business success. If one includes the foreign branches of industrial concerns, Liechtenstein has far more jobs than inhabitants. The country not only exports products and services, but also creates jobs abroad.

Unaxis Balzers supplies the key technologies for high-tech products such as digital data-storage devices, microchips and mobile phones.

Diversification – diversity of industries and products in a very small area

Hilti products and systems boost the productivity of construction professionals worldwide.

Hilti stands for innovation.

Hilti is a technology leader.

As an industrial location Liechtenstein has what it takes. In a very small area, in many cases within sight of one another, internationally successful business concerns are developing, producing and distributing quality branded products in demand from millions of people the world over. Many are unaware that these products and services originate in Liechtenstein. All the greater is the astonishment at the fact that key technologies for the IT sector and space travel come from Liechtenstein. Or that Liechtenstein companies are among the world's leaders in the market for construction and fastening equipment, crankshafts for the motor industry, connector systems for the entertainment industry and cosmetic materials for use in dentistry. The broad diversification across industries, enterprises and products is astonishing. It ranges from waste incineration plants and cut crystal to supplying convenience foods.

The quality of Hilti equipment explains its world reputation.

Hilti offers construction professionals worldwide innovative solutions with superior added value.
(Picture: Hilti Group headquarters in Schaan)

Ahead in knowledge – research and development are to the fore

At its headquarters in Schaan, Ivoclar Vivadent develops product systems for dentists and dental technicians.

Ivoclar Vivadent dental products are used in over 100 countries.

Industry and goods production provide almost half of the just under 30,000 jobs in Liechtenstein. This proportion is high in comparison with other western economies, where some 25 to 30 percent of employed persons work in the manufacturing industries. The small domestic market and the absence of state subsidies for trade and industry mean that concerns must maintain their position in international markets on the strength of their own resources. With their intensive research and development work, Liechtenstein's industrial enterprises lay the foundation for their strong position in worldwide competition. Technology transfer from the universities and colleges plays an important part in this. The export industry invests around CHF 300 million annually in research and development, equivalent to an outlay of more than CHF 8,000.00 per inhabitant.

Ivoclar Vivadent – market leader in materials for cosmetic dentistry.

Ivoclar Vivadent is a leading manufacturer of high-quality dental materials for preventive, restorative and prosthetic dentistry.

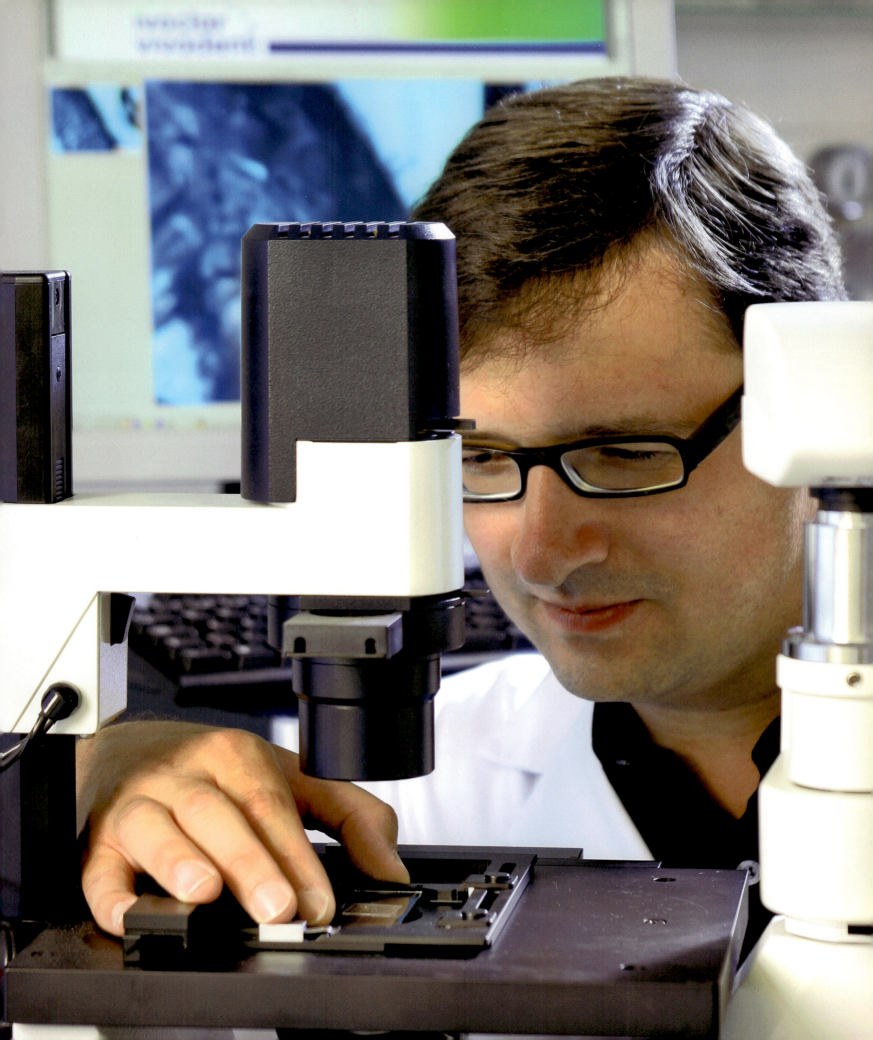

Internationality – membership of two economic areas

Fresh produce, frozen and tinned food reach the customers directly from production at Hilcona's headquarters in Schaan.

Since 1924 Liechtenstein and Switzerland have formed a single customs and currency union. The larger market and the Swiss franc have accelerated the country's economic development. Accession to the European Economic Area in 1995 created an unusual situation in that Liechtenstein has since belonged to two different economic areas. This is however a consequence of the country's liberal economic policy, which is aimed at giving business enterprises a favourable framework and unrestricted access to European markets. The technology centre and the highly developed financial centre have brought prosperity to the country. Liechtenstein is an important regional employer. Every day around 13,000 cross-border commuters come into the country to work. The strength of the economy is evident in the gross domestic product of CHF 4.2 billion.

Hilcona creates pasta dishes for the whole of Europe. The product mix reflects present-day eating habits and ranges from pizzas through soups and sauces to pre-cooked meals and fresh-daily sandwiches.

The gourmet convenience foods are devised and tested to perfection by professional cooks.

Orientation towards Switzerland – alignment in welfare and commercial law

The Ospelt Group in Bendern supplies markets all over Europe with its Malbun meat specialities, convenience products and high-quality animal foods.

The firm's founder Herbert Ospelt.

Close economic cooperation with Switzerland has led to numerous bilateral agreements. These among other things form the basis for the open frontier between the two states and for the use of the Swiss franc as official currency in Liechtenstein. This accounts for the fact that Swiss customs laws and Switzerland's customs agreements with outside states are applied in Liechtenstein too. The joint economic area has brought about alignment of statutory provisions in welfare and commercial law. These links are of great practical importance in national insurance and in indirect taxes. There are however common features in other areas as well, such as apprentice and vocational training and police cooperation.

The Ospelt Group's meat specialities are distinguished by innovative creations and love of quality.

Economic agreements – access to European markets

The Elkuch Group provides a comprehensive sheet-metal service.

In the lead worldwide: plate heat exchangers, developed and manufactured at Hoval.

Heating systems for traditional and alternative energy sources.

To secure access to the European markets for the country's export-oriented trade and industry, Liechtenstein has, in addition to the bilateral agreements with Switzerland, also concluded important multilateral agreements. The country has been a full member of the European Free Trade Association (EFTA) since 1991 and part of the European Economic Area (EEA) since 1995. Within the European Union's internal market, which under the EEA Agreement also includes Liechtenstein, the principle of free movement of goods, capital, services and persons applies, as does a common competition law. As an EEA state Liechtenstein adopts the European Union's internal market legislation into its national law. Excepted from this are taxes, agriculture, fisheries and trade policy.

Hoval stands for innovative heating systems, ventilation and process heat, and builds systems which meet the most exacting standards.

Value creation – strong industrialisation with a high export quota

ThyssenKrupp Presta in Eschen is one of the twelve most successful manufacturers of control systems worldwide, is the world market leader in assembled crankshafts and technology leader in the field of solid forming.

Financial services are less dominant in Liechtenstein's economy than is generally assumed. The value added by industry and the manufacturing trades accounts for some 40 percent of gross domestic product, while the share apportionable to financial services is 30 percent. The export industry forms an important pillar of economic success. It is present in the international markets with technologically top products. The per-capita value of annual export sales of more than five billion francs is approximately ten times higher than in Germany, Austria or Switzerland.

As innovative partners of the international motor industry ThyssenKrupp Presta have a technological lead in light-weight construction.

The technology supplied by ThyssenKrupp Presta contributes to making vehicles even more durable, safer, more economical and more comfortable.

Locational policy – liberal framework with a high level of self-responsibility

 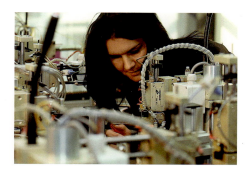 

Neutrik AG in Schaan is the leading manufacturer of plug connectors for the professional audio and video industry.

In the competition between business locations Liechtenstein scores well. Factors in its success are a tax quota low by international standards and a liberal economic policy, stability and dependability in the political field and in legislation, the high standard of training and the innovative power of a leading technology region. Simultaneous membership of the Swiss and European Economic Areas and membership of the World Trade Organisation (WTO) also operate in Liechtenstein's favour. The country establishes a favourable framework for entrepreneurial activities. Because of its smallness there is however in Liechtenstein no direct state assistance in the form of export subsidies for businesses.

The headquarters of Neutrik AG in Liechtenstein service a broad network of exclusive agencies providing technical support for customers in eighty countries.

The Neutrik Group has subsidiaries in North America, Great Britain, Germany, Switzerland, France, Japan and China.

Brands – visible tokens of Liechtenstein's quality work

Gifts and collectors' items made from artistically faceted crystal have made Swarovski famous.

The Swarovski logistics centre in Triesen.

More familiar than the company names are the brand names under which Liechtenstein products are distributed in the European markets and in some cases worldwide. These brands represent high-tech products of superlative quality. Liechtenstein is strongly represented in machine, equipment and plant construction and also in the dental and food industries. Exports by business enterprises belonging to the Liechtenstein Chamber of Commerce and Industry (LCCI) amount to some 5 billion francs. In Liechtenstein these industrial concerns employ barely a quarter of the people who work for them. Some 28,000 jobs are in the foreign branches. The great strength of these regionally and internationally interlinked concerns is the rapidity with which they respond to signals from the market.

Leading manufacturer worldwide of cut crystal.

The Austrian company group maintains a production site in Liechtenstein.

Small businesses – backbone of the economy

The efficient construction industry has adjusted its capacities to the sustained strong building activity of recent years.

Liechtenstein's economic structure is characterised by a high proportion of small and medium-sized businesses. Alongside the export industry and the financial services sector these form a third pillar of the country's highly diversified economy. The approximately 3,000 smaller business and service enterprises have, as regional providers and suppliers, a large share in the country's successful economic development. They provide a third of the 30,000 jobs in Liechtenstein. Many of these small businesses have found niche markets in which with acumen and entrepreneurial skill they hold their own in the international markets. By contrast sectors such as construction and retailing concentrate on the region. As a centre of expertise, training and employment Liechtenstein acts as a beacon across the border region, attracting large streams of commuters.

In the last few years the average annual volume of building work has reached about a million cubic metres.

3,000 industrial employers in very diverse sectors employ about a third of the workforce.

Apprentice training – job outlines in commerce and skilled trades

After leaving school, young people in Liechtenstein have a good chance of finding an apprenticeship in one of the country's many training companies.

Liechtenstein's concentration of specialist shops is notable. They are known for offering friendly, knowledgeable advice and a variety of products rarely found outside major centres.

Liechtenstein's industry trains young people in 95 skilled trades. The training concept, with a theoretical element at vocational school and the imparting of practical knowledge at the training centre, is based on the Swiss model. The variety of sectors represented in Liechtenstein means that traineeships are available in practically all industrial and commercial occupations. Since the introduction of the Berufsmatura (vocational high school degree), vocational training has become markedly more attractive as an alternative to an academic career. An indication of the high standard of training is the fact that Liechtenstein participants regularly win top scores in the WorldSkills Championships and return to Liechtenstein with medals.

Garden centres and floristry outlets «flourish» and attract many customers and visitors with their superbly colourful displays.

Intersection points – international flows of finance

Political and legal stability form the financial centre's foundation.

Privacy is a highly-valued asset in Liechtenstein's concept of the state.

The myth of a financial paradise which attracts foreign capital unchecked in astronomical amounts solely by virtue of its liberal tax and company law belongs to the past. Liechtenstein is one of the intersection points in the international flow of finance because it epitomises values such as stability and trust and can demonstrate relative advantages in an international comparison of locations. These are however not confined to the attractive tax system. A central role is played by the high quality of financial services and the protection of the client's privacy by banking secrecy. The fact that in legal protection of personality and liberal management of the economy Liechtenstein applies the same standards at home as in international business, has contributed substantially to the centre's credibility.

The Liechtensteinische Landesbank, founded in 1861, is the most traditional of Liechtenstein's 15 banks.

Financial centre – asset management, investment and insurance

The world's most important rating agencies give the Liechtenstein financial centre the highest score, the AAA national rating.

The financial services sector in Liechtenstein employs some 4,000 people and contributes about thirty percent, or 1.3 billion francs, to the gross domestic product (GDP). With professionalism and attractive general conditions the financial centre has focused on private asset management, international asset structuring and in recent years increasingly on investment funds and insurance. With fifteen banks, more than a hundred investment undertakings and over twenty insurance companies, it is an important part of the Liechtenstein economy, and yet by international standards relatively small. Nor, with thirteen percent of the working population, is it the country's largest business sector, as is often assumed abroad. Industry and the manufacturing trades, which provide forty-five percent of the approximately 30,000 jobs in Liechtenstein, are the major elements.

Expertise in private banking.

Strict laws on investor protection generate confidence.

The LGT Bank unites the financial experts of the Princely House of Liechtenstein. At 29 first-rate locations in Europe, the Middle and Far East and America they provide their clients with comprehensive wealth management.

Banking secrecy – part of Liechtenstein's concept of the state

Many years' experience, discretion and high quality standards distinguish Liechtenstein financial service undertakings.

Combination of architectural distinction and the financial world: the Centrum Bank building in Vaduz.

The confidential relationship between banker and client is an expression of Liechtenstein's concept of the state, according to which protection of privacy is a highly-valued asset in the relationship between citizen and state. This basic approach provides both citizens and clients of the Liechtenstein financial centre with a guarantee that their personal integrity will be respected. The unavoidable risk of criminal misuse of financial services has been countered by Liechtenstein with a new law on mutual legal assistance in criminal matters and toughened provisions on due diligence. Introduction of financial market supervision independent of the state and strengthening of the enforcement authorities in personnel terms ensure effective combating of crime. These clear signals have been acknowledged by the international organisations and have further enhanced the overall attractiveness of the financial centre.

The VP Bank in Vaduz is one of the leading private banks with an international orientation.

Agriculture – ideas and the best milk in Europe

Relocated farms in the agricultural area are the counterpart to the many small landholdings used for farming purposes in the valley area and to alpine farming.

Cows descend from the alpine pastures.

The area in agricultural use covers a little under a quarter of the country's 16,000 hectares. Milk production is the principal income source in the primary sector, which now employs only one percent of Liechtenstein's working population. The climatic and topographical conditions lend themselves especially well to fodder cropping. The annual milk production of some 14,000 tonnes is sufficient to cover Liechtenstein's own needs. The farmers' income losses due to the livelihood-jeopardising collapse of prices are to some extent made up for by direct payments from the state. Original marketing ideas and a milk quality awarded the gold accolade against European competition promote sales of home-produced dairy products.

Cheese production is a sideline for the farmers.

Wooden hearts in gratitude for a loss-free alpine summer.

The milk's outstanding quality plays a decisive part in its processing into sought-after fresh dairy products for the regional market.

Organic products – ecological and market-oriented

Harvesting of sugar beet and processing of maize into silage are images from everyday rural life in Liechtenstein.

Technology and nature characterise the farmer's work.

The Rhine valley's mild climate with an average temperature over the year of 9°C is influenced by the föhn, a hot dry wind. The warm south wind causes substantial rises in temperature, mainly in the spring and autumn. This has a favourable effect on the vegetation and above all on the growing of maize and wine. The confined agricultural areas between Liechtenstein's mountain regions and the Rhine are used mainly for market gardening and fodder cropping. The low-impact and natural form of cultivation and direct selling of organic products improve the economic basis of many farmers. 1100 hectares are under cultivation for growing crops, vegetables, fruit and wine and a further 2400 hectares of farmland and 2000 hectares of alpine meadow are used for meat and milk production.

Integrated production and organic cultivation secure the market-gardeners' livelihood. Their high-quality organic produce sells well.

Winegrowing – princely drops in a rural ambience

A superb Pinot noir growing in the Prince's Vineyard in the Vaduz domain.

The wines are stored in oak casks.

Labels embellished with Princely coat-of-arms.

With its slopes, mild climate and fertile, calcareous soils Liechtenstein is traditionally a winegrowing area. Today over 20 different grape varieties grow on 26 hectares in use for winegrowing. The Blauburgunder is the most important representative of the blue grape, the Riesling x Sylvaner the most extensively planted white grape. The country's approximately 100 winegrowers also however cultivate varieties such as Blaufränkisch, Zweigelt, Regent and Maréchal Foch or Chardonnay, Pinot blanc and Pinot gris, Gewürztraminer, Seyval blanc, Saphira and Bianca. Most of the harvested grapes are pressed in Liechtenstein. In good years the entire harvest from Liechtenstein's vineyards, which are located on south- to west-facing areas of debris cones resulting from erosion and on the slopes of the Eschnerberg, yields wine output of over 100,000 litres, bought mainly in the local region.

Direct sale in the Prince's wine cellars.

Wine harvest on the Eschnerberg. In Liechtenstein quality wines are produced according to the latest findings from viticultural research.

Haute Cuisine – creative and highly decorated chefs

The country's sophisticated catering celebrates a refined gastronomic culture and pampers its guests with culinary delights.

Elegant restaurants with atmosphere.

The guild of Liechtenstein top chefs has grown larger. In the last few years the flagship of Liechtenstein's haute cuisine, the widely acclaimed Restaurant Real, has been joined by a number of establishments offering creative and distinguished cuisine. International cooking, with seasonal dishes of outstanding quality, is done with a perfection which has already elicited words of delight from a number of restaurant critics. With their exquisite service and a wine-list which surprises even experts the elegant restaurants are among the region's leading establishments. The gastronomic delights on offer flatter palate and tongue in equal measure and become, thanks to the elegant atmosphere, an overall experience which delights again and again both residents and visitors from the locality.

The country's much decorated leading gastronomic providers with pioneer Felix Real are known for their high-quality cuisine and polished service.

Specialities – plain cooking in the country inns

Freshly cooked cheese dumplings are a traditional Liechtenstein speciality served in some restaurants.

Eating cheese dumplings in congenial company is popular with the people of Liechtenstein.

Typical Liechtenstein specialities are few in number, but all the more nutritious for that. The earlier national dishes arose not from any Liechtenstein cuisine as such, but were part of the basic diet of the people of the Rhineland. They included for example Rhine valley white maize. The maize dishes made from it were and are a regional speciality, but one which is now almost unobtainable in inns and restaurants. There is however on the menu of some country inns another Liechtenstein delicacy, the popular «Käsknöpfle» or cheese dumplings. They are served according to taste and custom with either apple and elderberry sauce or with potato salad and in any event with a lot of fried onions. Among the dishes in the original rustic cooking are also potato noodles and other potato and pastry dishes.

With their comfortable atmosphere the homely country inns enrich the gastronomic choice on offer with their plain simple cuisine.

Scene – fashionable restaurants and much more

As meeting points, for a glass or cappuccino, there is a colourful mixture of pubs, bistros and cafés to choose from.

Liechtenstein's young people meet to chat and socialize.

The men and of course also the women of Liechtenstein are sociable people who relate closely to one another. In their spare time many of them are active in one of the country's many clubs. They are the cement which enlivens the village community and promotes social cohesion. They are however also an important part of social life in Liechtenstein. Like-minded people meet up for shared use of their leisure time and for good companionship in one of the country's many hospitable bars. There items of news are exchanged, the political situation discussed, opinions formed and often the major festivals celebrated unplanned. Preferred meeting points are the various fashionable restaurants, the apéro bar and of course the homely village inn, where the landlord still attends to the guests' well-being in person.

An evening out or an excursion often leads to one of the country's distinctive apéro bars.

Country of culture – a wealth of forms of cultural expression

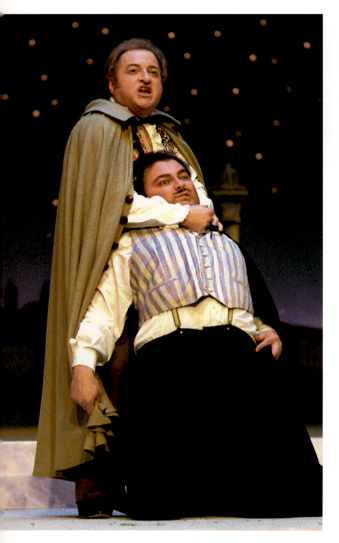

The country's operetta stages have a long tradition.

Films and music are permanent features of the varied cultural events on offer in Liechtenstein.

National identity is reflected in the common origin and in maintenance of the cultural heritage. Christian basic values and different influences resulting from the country's position on a major north-south communication route are expressed in customs and in inherited traditions. As part of the cultural landscape of the Lake Constance area exchange with other people and other ideas is a distinctive element in Liechtenstein's self-image. The small state cooperates with Europe and the region not just in political and economic matters, but also in the cultural field. This stimulating interaction of different cultures and cultural encounters rank high in Liechtenstein. The country of culture encourages diversity of cultural expression and knows how to engage its own cultural output in dialogue with the regional and international cultural scene.

Liechtenstein's cabaret show, LiGa.

The Theater am Kirchplatz in Schaan with its distinguished programme enjoys an excellent reputation and attracts patrons from all over the region.

Artists – reflecting Liechtenstein's soul

In the Engländerbau arts centre contemporary artists feature in exhibitions, installations, readings and performances.

Some of Liechtenstein's artists have also made names for themselves abroad. The plastic works of Georg Malin (above) and the sculptures of Hugo Marxer attract international attention.

Contemporary creative art in Liechtenstein has many facets. One which attracts attention beyond the country's borders is fine and applied art. Some of the country's 50 or so painters and sculptors have made names for themselves internationally. The country encourages artistic endeavour by means of exchange schemes and annual work grants, by purchasing works by Liechtenstein artists and by providing premises for exhibitions. In the Liechtenstein art and culture landscape all the other arts such as music, film, theatre, dance and literature are however also represented. Among the best-known cultural institutions are the Kunstmuseum Liechtenstein and the National Museum in Vaduz and the Theater am Kirchplatz in Schaan. On the country's beautiful stamps national and international artists reflect Liechtenstein themes.

Among the handicrafts represented in Liechtenstein is the making of paper in the craft workshops of Hanspeter Leibold.

A jewel – atmosphere, art and encounter under one roof

The Kunstmuseum Liechtenstein concept meets with great approval with specialists and art connoisseurs from inside and outside Liechtenstein.

The key focus in the collection of the Kunstmuseum Liechtenstein is on 19th and 20th century works of art. As the second important collection in Liechtenstein it thus augments and extends the time horizon of the Princely Collections, which include works of art from late mediaeval times into the 19th century. The Kunstmuseum Liechtenstein concentrates on a thematically oriented collecting policy in the fields sculpture/object/installation, plastic and other three-dimensional works together with graphic works. It displays temporary exhibitions on art since 1900 and presents the items in its collection on the «dialogue» principle. The Museum is an architectural jewel with rooms full of atmosphere, which stimulate visitors to discover art.

For many visitors to the Principality of Liechtenstein a stay in the country is incomplete without a visit to the exhibition rooms of the Kunstmuseum Liechtenstein.

The exhibitions at the Kunstmuseum Liechtenstein are of high quality and are enthusiastically praised by an international public.

Origin – in close touch with one's own past

The Liechtenstein National Museum presents in Vaduz a thematically organised permanent exhibition focused on human activities. Under the six key concepts «settlement», «protection», «rule», «celebration», «creativity» and «use of resources» these activities are brought into an overall context. The collections of the Liechtenstein National Museum include objects from the history of Liechtenstein and the region. Since 2003 the National Museum has shown exhibits from the Natural History Collections of the Principality of Liechtenstein in addition to its own natural-history items – with special regional emphasis on the ornithology, botany and fauna and flora of the Alpine region. The National Museum additionally maintains a Farmhouse Museum in Schellenberg.

First map of Liechtenstein by Jacob Heber, dating from 1721.

Imperial Charter on Liechtenstein's elevation to Imperial Principality in 1719.

The well-preserved late 16th century Farmhouse Room in the National Museum gives an insight into how earlier generations lived.

Settlement dating from the Neolithic period (4000–1800 BC) is attested.

The Lenten cloth from Bendern parish church was made in 1612. It depicts scenes from the Old and New Testaments.

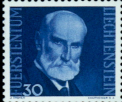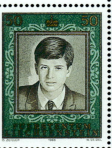

Quality of life – recreation on the doorstep

Hikes in the Liechtenstein Mountain Region are very rewarding in terms of relaxation and discovery. Many mountain walkers take a break at the Pfälzerhütte.

The Gänglesee in Steg is one of the popular destinations for family outings with children.

Liechtenstein is notable less for spectacular buildings and historical village scenes than for its large extent of recreational landscape. The Mountain Regions extend over two-thirds of the country. The mountain scenery in the east of the country, including the well-known Three Sisters Massif, forms a natural barrier between the Rhine valley and the Alpine high valleys. Lofty peaks up to 2600 metres high, inviting mountain trails and many rewarding places to visit offer rest and recreation. Attractions in the valley are the water-meadow and marsh landscapes, the Rhine and the Eschnerberg, which rises like an island in the Rhine valley to a good 650 metres. From the wetlands of the Ruggell marsh to the high mountains of the Falknis Group walkers and climbers come into contact with nature in its most varied and beautiful manifestations.

The leisure facilities in the local communities provide exercise and relaxation for all ages.

Movement – sports, leisure and recreation in Liechtenstein

Mountain-bikers have a wide choice of valley and mountain trails.

Recreation for people and animals by the Rhine.

He who wants out at the top will find a wall.

More than a third of Liechtenstein's population practise one or more sports in the country's well over a hundred sports clubs. Love of sport in Liechtenstein also manifests itself in the lavishly laid out sports and leisure facilities such as the Rheinpark Stadium in Vaduz, a modern small stadium in which Liechtenstein's national football team plays its home matches and FC Vaduz competes for the championship in the second-highest Swiss football league. Other showpieces are the athletics centre in Schaan, the discovery park in the Mühleholz swimming-pool area and the Eschen-Mauren sports ground. In almost all the country's local communities and at school centres there are attractive sports facilities. Many residents combine light exercise with discovering nature at one of the many local recreation areas: on foot, by bike or on in-line skates. On pleasant days some 400 kilometres of hiking and cycling trails in the mountain regions and in the valley draw thousands of nature- and sport-loving people.

Mühleholz Leisure Park with one of the region's finest open-air swimming pools.

Football is one of the most popular team games in Liechtenstein.

Family paradise – discovery and sport in snowbound nature

Downhill run from the Sareiserjoch with slopes of various degrees of difficulty takes beginners and experienced skiers safely into the valley.

Again and again individual sportsmen from Liechtenstein manage the leap to top status in the world. The good results in alpine and nordic skiing delight and astonish, especially since the country is one of the smallest skiing and cross-country skiing nations. There has been much speculation as to the reasons for the above-average success rate. Individual encouragement of talent, a professional training scheme with cross-border cooperation, much self-discipline and strong motivation to deliver peak performance are important factors. Even more important however is sheer delight in sport, which Liechtenstein's young people acquire as it were by «inoculation» when they first attempt to move around in the magnificent scenery of the Malbun-Steg winter sports area.

Liechtenstein is investing in a modern and attractive infrastructure in the family-friendly Malbun-Steg winter sports area.

In Malbun-Steg winter sportsmen and those seeking recreation find cross-country ski-trails, ski-runs, tobogganing and hiking trails in an untouched winter landscape.

Rhine culture – a land and its river as characterising elements

The last covered wooden bridge on the river frontier with Switzerland links Vaduz with Sevelen. All other wooden bridges have been destroyed by fire.

The point where the Inland Canal flows into the Rhine at Ruggell is one of the popular local recreation areas in the countryside.

Landscapes of exquisite beauty, jewels of nature, a paradise for earthbound human beings. Small though Liechtenstein is, the populated area is much smaller still, wherein lies the clue to the country's true wealth: it is generously endowed with untouched stretches of countryside, with forests, mountain ranges and alpine pastures, with marshy landscapes and water-meadows. The dominance of the world of mountains and alpine pastures is challenged only by the rule of the Alpine Rhine, which gave its name to the valley and forms the natural border with Switzerland. The Liechtenstein Mountain Regions cover two-thirds of the country's area. The Alps are among the most beautiful sights Liechtenstein has to offer. Anyone walking one of the over 400-kilometres long mountain trails is met again and again by fascinating new vistas.

From the Walser community of Triesenberg there is an extensive view over the Rhine valley.

Historic buildings – enduring witnesses to the past

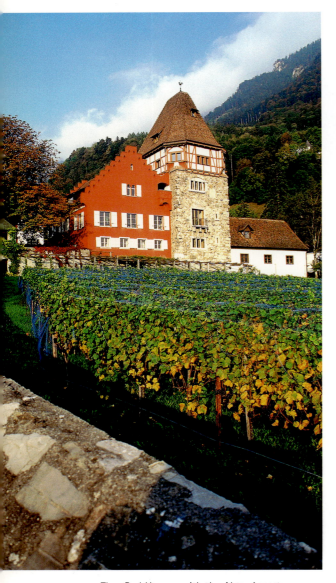

The «Red House» with the Abtswingert (Abbey Vineyard) above Vaduz.

The historically important church hill at Bendern.

Gutenberg Castle in Balzers-Mäls.

Castle ruin, Schellenberg.

Scenic delights are not confined to the Alpine region. A visitor to one of the eleven small local communities soon comes outside the centres upon oases of tranquillity in the countryside and witnesses to the rustic past and its style of building. Historic buildings and monuments from bygone times recall a history remote from the affluence of today and also from the romance we like to see in the past. The olden days were characterised by a slower pace of life which today we seem to have lost. Anyone with a little time to spare who slows down for a moment is richly rewarded. This leisure sharpens the eye for what constitutes Liechtenstein's appeal: landscapes which radiate tranquillity, away from the heavily used roads and popular spots, structural witnesses to times past and symbols of inherited traditions next to elegant office facades.

The chapel of the Holy Cross at Rofenberg in Eschen was the former Lordship of Schellenberg's place of execution.

View of the southernmost community Balzers with Gutenberg Castle, which rises above the valley floor on a mound some seventy metres high.

Architecture – dramatic contrasts of rustic and urban

Offices in green surroundings.

Apartment blocks are growing apace.

The tranquil village square of Schellenberg with its modern parish church.

The form of settlement and the architectural contrasts mark an image often encountered in Liechtenstein. Structures typical of the village combine with urban elements. Ultramodern architecture, forms of building and facades mingle with the traditional. Such village views reveal much about the nature of Liechtenstein people, who are open to new ideas without having lost their attachment to the soil. The simple method of construction and way of life of bygone times contrast with today's high standard of finish and technical functionality. Herein it is perhaps most strikingly evident how rapidly Liechtenstein's change from agrarian to industrial and service economy only a few decades ago has brought affluence to the country and its people. Liechtenstein has a high proportion of houses in single occupation, which are very popular with the people. The shortage of land and high property prices mean however that more and more people live in apartment blocks, which sometimes form entirely new districts.

Diversity of architectural styles.

Harmony and tension between old and new characterise the view of Vaduz Castle from the front of the Kunstmuseum Liechtenstein.

The community of Triesen is considered the country's oldest self-contained settlement. Above the village are vineyards and the historic chapel of St. Mamertus.

Geography – favoured situation and land as a scarce commodity

The rural buildings, often neat flower-decked wooden houses, are a record of earlier construction methods and the rustic past.

View of a group of houses and the chapel dedicated to St. Joseph in Planken, the smallest community in Liechtenstein with 400 inhabitants.

Liechtenstein lies between latitude 47° 16' and 47° 03' north and between longitude 9° 28' and 9° 38' east of Greenwich. At its greatest it is 24.6 kilometres long and 12.4 kilometres wide. Of its territory of 160 square kilometres 42 percent are forested, 34 percent used agriculturally and 15 percent unproductive. The populated area covers some 14 square kilometres or 9 percent. The territorial smallness expressed in this highlights the fact that land is a scarce commodity in Liechtenstein, unevenly distributed moreover over the eleven communities. The community with the largest area is Triesenberg at 29.8 square kilometres, that with the smallest Schellenberg at 3.5 square kilometres. The confined circumstances call for far-sighted zone and regional planning at both national and local level.

Scene from the pedestrianised zone in the centre of Vaduz, which attracts tourists from all over the world.

Traditions – roots of identity

The burning of the beacon and the capers at Shrovetide are firmly embedded traditions.

Procession in the Mauren community.

Old customs and inherited traditions are kept up in Liechtenstein. The colourful Shrovetide carnival, which culminates in the days leading up to Ash Wednesday. Beacon Sunday, the first Sunday in Lent, with the burning of a large pile of wood with the Beacon Witch on top. The Feast of the Assumption and the National Holiday on 15th August. The Feast of Corpus Christi with solemn processions past lovingly decked altars. Secular and ecclesiastical customs have their firm place in the yearly cycle. There are unmistakable influences from other cultural groups, which combine the traditional with newer features. An example of these are the Halloween parties, held around All Saints' Day, at a time traditionally devoted to remembrance and thoughts of the departed.

Many of Liechtenstein's associations are active in the cultural field and provide a festive framework for church and secular occasions.

Local autonomy – self-determination for the local authorities

Schaan as one of the region's major business locations has been able to preserve its rural character with high-quality housing.

Liechtenstein's Constitution enshrines four cardinal principles: the monarchic principle, the democratic principle, the rule of law and the principle of local autonomy. The important part played in the state by the local communities is linked closely to their independence (autonomy) in their own sphere of activity. This includes election of community authorities, organisation of the community, conferment of civil rights, administration of community assets and erection of public buildings and facilities, together with collection of community charges and setting of tax surcharges. The communities' own revenue from community charges, subsidies and fiscal equalisation form an important basis for the exercise of local autonomy.

Art is ever-present on a stroll through Vaduz.

Seat of the community administration at Mauren Town Hall.

One of the sights at Vaduz, the capital of Liechtenstein, is the Town Hall, which houses the mayor's office and community administration.

View from the mountain community of Planken over the mist-streaked Rhine valley and the Eschnerberg. The massive rock formations of the Swiss Kreuzberge can be seen in the background.

Houses of God – sacred buildings and symbols of faith

The Chapel of St. Mary at Masescha dates back to the early 14th century. In the interior of the distinctive building there are impressive fragments of the original murals.

Predominantly Roman Catholic, Liechtenstein was for some 1600 years part of the Bishopric of Chur. In 1997 His Holiness Pope John Paul II, who had visited the country twelve years previously on 8th September 1985, established the Archdiocese of Vaduz by the Apostolic Constitution «Ad satius consulendum». The Archdiocese has since then been directly subordinate to the Holy See, with which the Principality established official diplomatic relations in 1985. The history of the church is essentially the history of the parishes and establishments of the religious Orders. Today some three-quarters of the population belong to the Roman Catholic Church. Liechtenstein's national patron saint is St. Lucius, apostle and martyr, who was a missionary in the Chur area in earliest times (probably before 700).

The solemn procession at Corpus Christi and the First Communion on Whitsunday are high points in the cycle of the church's year.

The Chapel of St. Maria zum Trost, consecrated in 1743 at Dux in Schaan has a largely original baroque interior.

Patronage – Princely support in hard times

Modern village square with the parish church of St. Martin and the Pfrundhaus in Eschen.

The Princely Family assisted the communities financially in the building of churches. Examples are Eschen parish church, reflected in the village fountain, and the parish church of St. Laurence in Schaan.

The relations which have evolved between the Princely House of Liechtenstein and the country's local communities are complex and traditional. One factor contributing to the mutual commitment was generous princely donations to public institutions and building projects in the 19th and early 20th centuries, above all in the reign of Prince Johann II (1840–1929) with his notable commitment in the social welfare and humanitarian field. It is from this time that several of the country's parish churches date, built with assistance from the Prince. They are tokens of a devout population which commended the country to God's protection in hard times. For Liechtenstein's history has been dogged by the three «national scourges» mud- and rock-slides, foehn and Rhine. From time immemorial the people of the Rhine valley have treated these natural forces with great respect.

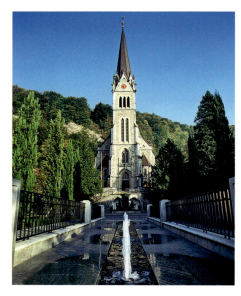

View of the parish church in Vaduz, now elevated to cathedral status.

The parish church at Ruggell symbolises the people's belief in God's protection against the forces of nature.

The plant conservation area in the Ruggell marsh with its incomparable flora and the glowing lily-fields is a natural paradise familiar far beyond the national frontiers.

Moods – magic of the winter landscapes in the Rhine valley

For Liechtensteiners and many visitors winter in Liechtenstein is synonymous with glorious winter sports and encounters with nature in the Alpine region of Steg-Malbun. On some days in the cold season the sunlit heights offer a very special experience of nature when they open up a view of the sea of mist in the valley. The cultivated landscapes of the Rhine plain are transformed into magical and seemingly untouched winter landscapes. When the snow covers up the traces of human activity, the loveliest time for extended winter walks has come. The onset of winter often comes as a surprise, too early for many, too late for others. It brings joy above all to children and winter-sports enthusiasts.

In the valley area too winter in Liechtenstein provides impressive natural phenomena.

Sunrise in the wintry Rhine landscape.

Winter impressions from the northern view of the Castle, dominated by the mighty belfry and the north round bastion.

The snow-covered Swiss mountains are reflected in Gamprin Mere, an unspoilt natural biotope between the communities of Gamprin and Ruggell.

The scenic beauty of the Ruggell marsh combines with a panorama of the mountain chain in neighbouring Switzerland, radiant in the evening sun.

Werdenberg – neighbour with a past

Timber and stone facades form narrow alleys.

The nearby castle and town of Werdenberg bear witness to a past rich in the history of civilisation. Above the town, the oldest timber-built settlement in Switzerland and worth seeing in its own right, sits the castle, accessible only via a footpath. The former family seat of the Counts of Werdenberg today houses a Museum of the Home with well-preserved residential quarters furnished in the Biedermeier style, a collection of weapons and an exhibition on the history of the St. Gallen Canton. From the castle tower there is a magnificent panoramic view of the Rhine valley. Many visitors stroll through the narrow streets of the historic town enjoying the superbly preserved architectural monuments, which transport the onlooker back to a bygone age. Other magnets for the public are cultural events such as the Castle Festival and the Regional Museum in the Schlangenhaus.

The historic groups of houses are rich in decorative elements and picturesque corners.

Lake Buchs with the town of Werdenberg and the castle of the same name cast their spell over the visitor.

Feldkirch – atmosphere of a fascinating mediaeval town

The romantic Old Town of Feldkirch with its many arcades has charm and atmosphere.

The first documentary mention of the town of Feldkirch dates from 1218. Many architectural monuments in the romantic Old Town, centuries-old towers and town houses bear witness to by-gone ages. Schattenburg Castle, symbol of the mediaeval town of Feldkirch, was built in the 12th century. Hugo I von Montfort used it to guard the town and traffic over the passes leading south and east. The hidden corners in the attractive pedestrianised zone with their tranquil arcades make the town of the Montforts a popular destination for excursions. The busy alleys and squares of the town centre are the setting for numerous events. Farmers' markets are held here every week.

In the well-preserved mediaeval heart of the town are the shops and the market-square of Feldkirch as a shopping centre.

Ardetzenberg Game Park gives an insight into the life of wild animals.

The mighty castle with its unique inner courtyard forms the atmosphere-filled setting for the comfortable and friendly Castle Restaurant.

Maienfeld – tranquil town in the Canton of Grisons

Maienfeld, the principal town of the Bündner Herrschaft and well worth seeing with its historic buildings, is surrounded by vineyards.

Winegrowing has a long tradition.

Area above Fläsch in which Maienfeld «Beerliwein» is grown.

Together with the communities of Fläsch, Jenins and Malans Maienfeld belongs to the Bündner Herrschaft, a part of Grisons which borders Liechtenstein in the south. The adjoining areas were once united with one another under the Barons of Brandis. The picturesque little town of Maienfeld is a popular excursion destination. The well-preserved historic buildings amid the vineyards are worth a visit. Maienfeld is known for its excellent «Beerliwein» and as the venue for the International Equestrian Festival. Liechtenstein's neighbour has however achieved world renown as the setting for the world-famous Heidi story by Johanna Spyri. In 1388 there is mention of a tollgate, indicating that a toll was collected at Maienfeld for use of the old Roman road leading northwards from Chur through Liechtenstein. Maienfeld Castle, now Brandis Castle, belonged originally to the Counts of Bregenz. The castle came to the Barons of Brandis by inheritance in 1438.

The spa town of Bad Ragaz, well-known for its thermal springs.

The well-known Heidi Fountain recalls the world-famous story by Johanna Spyri.

Bibliography

Edmund Banzer, Georg Burgmeier, Norbert Bürzle, Luzius Malin. Fürst und Volk – Eine liechtensteinische Staatskunde. Schulamt des Fürstentums Liechtenstein (Hrsg.) 1993.

Hubert Büchel, Egon Gstöhl, Felix Näscher, Julius Ospelt. Fürstentum Liechtenstein. BuchsDruck und Verlag 1986.

Fürstenhaus Liechtenstein. Internetportal www.fuerstenhaus.li (2005).

Adulf Peter Goop, Günther Meier, Daniel Quaderer. Brauchtum Liechtenstein – Alte Bräuche und neue Sitten. Alpenland Verlag (Hrsg.) 2004.

Volker Press. Das Haus Liechtenstein in der europäischen Geschichte. In: Liechtenstein – Fürstliches Haus und staatliche Ordnung. V. Press / D. Willoweit (Hrsg.). Verlag der Liechtensteinischen Akademischen Gesellschaft 1987.

Rupert Quaderer. Die Entwicklung der liechtensteinischen Volksrechte seit 1818 bis zum Revolutionsjahr 1848. In: Liechtensteinische Politische Schriften Nr. 8. Verlag der Liechtensteinischen Akademischen Gesellschaft 1981.

Regierung des Fürstentums Liechtenstein. Landtag, Regierung und Gerichte 2004. Regierung des Fürstentums Liechtenstein (Hrsg.) 2005.

Regierung und Landesverwaltung. Internetportale www.llv.li und www.liechtenstein.li (2005).

Regierungssekretariat, Rechtsdienst der Regierung, Amt für auswärtige Angelegenheiten, Presse- und Informationsamt, Steuerverwaltung. Fürstentum Liechtenstein – Eine Dokumentation. Staat, Monarchie, Politik. Presse- und Informationsamt (Hrsg.) 2003. Available in English: Principality of Liechtenstein – A documentary account. State, monarchy, political system.

Otto Seger. Lachendes Liechtenstein. Selbstverlag 1982.

Otto Seger. Überblick über die liechtensteinische Geschichte. Presse- und Informationsamt der Regierung (Hrsg.) 1984.

Paul Vogt. 125 Jahre Landtag. Landtag des Fürstentums Liechtenstein (Hrsg.) 1987.

Paul Vogt. Brücken zur Vergangenheit. Schulamt des Fürstentums Liechtenstein 1990.

Herbert Wille. Die Verfassung von 1921: Parteien und Kirche. In: Das Fürstentum Liechtenstein. Veröffentlichung des Alemannischen Instituts Freiburg i. Br. Nr. 50. Wolfgang Müller (Hrsg.) 1981.

Landmarks in Liechtenstein history

100,000–15,000 BC Last ice age. The glaciers (Rhine glacier) shape the valleys.

10,000 BC Major rockslide in the Triesenberg-Triesen area.

From 4,000 BC Neolithic period. First settlers attested on Eschnerberg (Lutzengütle) and Gutenberg. Original population are Rhaetians; Celtic influences also discernible.

15 BC Rhaetia becomes a Roman province. Road-building through the Rhine valley.

From 6th/7th century Influx of Alemanni. Rhaetio-Romans and Alemanni exist alongside one another.

768–1806 Part of the Holy Roman Empire.

1342 Division of the County of Sargans brings about the County of Vaduz, whose owner also receives part of Eschnerberg.

1416 County of Vaduz comes under the rule of the Barons of Brandis.

1434 Barons of Brandis purchase the remainder of Eschnerberg. Territory of the present-day Principality united for the first time.

1699 Prince Johann Adam Andreas von Liechtenstein acquires the Lordship of Schellenberg for 115,000 gulden.

1712 Johann Adam acquires the County of Vaduz for 290,000 gulden.

1719 The County of Vaduz and Lordship of Schellenberg are elevated to become the Imperial Principality of Liechtenstein.

1806 Liechtenstein is included in the Confederation of the Rhine as a sovereign state.

1815 Liechtenstein becomes a sovereign member of the German Confederation.

1818 Absolutist constitution. Parliament of the Estates as precursor of a parliamentary system.

1848 Year of revolutions. The people demand more rights and liberties.

1852 Customs treaty with Austria.

1862 Constitution. Status of Landtag (Parliament) raised. Various liberties guaranteed.

1866 Dissolution of the German Confederation. Last deployment of the Liechtenstein army at Stilfserjoch.

1868 Abolition of the Liechtenstein army.

1914–1918 First World War. Liechtenstein remains neutral, suffers famine and high unemployment, is financially and economically ruined.

1918 «Liechtenstein for the Liechtensteiners» movement. Formation of the «People's Party» (since 1936 the «Patriotic Union») and «Progressive Citizens' Party».

1920 Postal Agreement with Switzerland.

1921 Written Constitution on a democratic and parliamentary foundation. A People's Principality comes into being.

1923 Customs treaty with Switzerland. Swiss franc becomes legal currency.

1938 Prince Franz Josef II is the first Prince to take up residence at Vaduz Castle.

1939–1945 Second World War. Liechtenstein is not directly involved in the hostilities. Food rationing and wartime economy. Great influx of refugees after the war.

1950 Membership of the International Court of Justice at The Hague.

Since 1952 Development of the welfare state. Old-age and survivors' insurance (1952), family allowances (1957), disability insurance (1959), income support (1965), unemployment insurance (1969), improvements in accident and sickness insurance.

1960 Association with the European Free Trade Area (EFTA), full member from 1991.

1972 Agreement with the European Economic Community (EC).

1975 Accession to the Organisation for Security and Cooperation in Europe (OSCE).

1978 Accession to the Council of Europe.

1990 Accession to the United Nations Organisation (UNO).

1995 Accession to the European Economic Area (EEA) Agreement.

Accession to the World Trade Organisation (WTO).

2003 New Constitution comes into force with various amendments to the dualistic combination of monarchy and democracy.

www.liechtenstein.li

Stabsstelle für Kommunikation und Öffentlichkeitsarbeit
(Government Spokesperson's Office)
Regierungsgebäude (Government Building)
FL-9490 Vaduz
Tel. +423 776 61 80
office@liechtenstein.li

www.tourismus.li

Liechtenstein Tourism
Städtle 37
PO Box 139
FL-9490 Vaduz
Tel. +423 239 63 00
Fax +423 239 63 01
info@tourismus.li